Just Joking 6

Get ready for
more
LAUGHS!

Just Joking 6

NATIONAL GEOGRAPHIC
KiDS

300 hilarious jokes about everything, including tongue twisters, riddles, and more!

Rosie Gowsell Pattison

NATIONAL GEOGRAPHIC
WASHINGTON, D.C.

KNOCK, KNOCK.
Who's there?
Nuttin'.
Nuttin' who?
Nuttin's going my way today.

4

Dinner's ready! Hyenas make a sound similar to a giggle. This sound tells other hyenas that they have food to share.
HA! HA! HA! HA! HA! HA!
5

Most geckos don't have eyelids. Instead they have clear membranes that they lick to keep clean.

TONGUE
TWISTER!
Say this fast three times:
Six sick
scenic
sightseers.

What do
you call a
nose with
no body?
Q
A
Nobody knows.

TONGUE TWISTER!

Say this fast three times:
Kristen's sister's biscuit mixer.

Where do pirates shop?
Q
At the maarrket.
A

What do you call an alligator eating Mexican food?
Q
A Taco-dile.
A

Q
Which superhero works at a dry cleaner in his spare time?
Iron Man.
A

Baby beluga whales are called calves. They are born gray or brown and turn white around five years old.

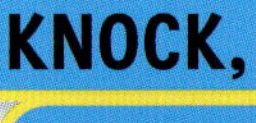

Lions are very social animals. They live in groups, called prides, of 15 or more.

Q What kind of bird recycles?
A A two-can.

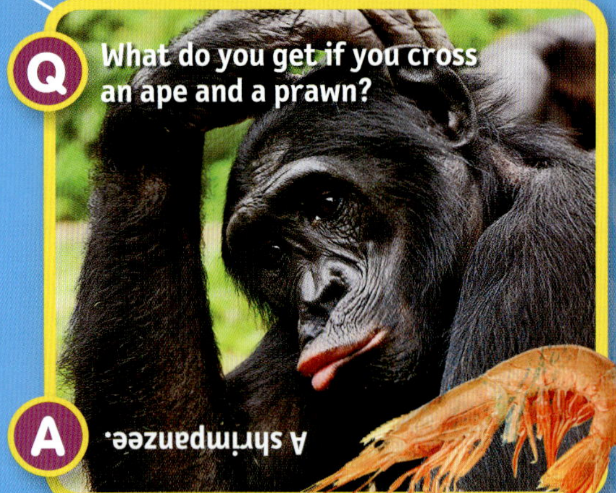

Q What do you get if you cross an ape and a prawn?
A A shrimpanzee.

Polar bears can weigh up to 1,200 pounds (544 kg) and can reach heights of 10 feet (3 m) tall when standing on their hind legs!

What do snowmen eat for breakfast?
Snowflakes.

TONGUE TWISTER!
Say this fast three times:
Sneaker speakers.

Q
What do you call a frog with no legs?
A
Unhoppy.

Q
What do you get if you cross a slice of bread and a bloodsucking bug?
A
Mosqui-toast.

Q
What was the fastest dinosaur?
A
A prontosaurus.

TONGUE
TWISTER!

Say this fast three times:

Bamboo
baboon.

The name "orangutan" means "person of the forest."
KNOCK, KNOCK.
Who's there?
Nana.
Nana who?
Nana your business!

18

Q
Why did the policeman give the gardener a ticket?
A
For disturbing the peas.

TONGUE TWISTER!
Say this fast three times:
Extinct insects.

Q How did the cheddar cheese feel after its vacation?

A It felt grate!

Q What kind of **lunch** do you get in the **desert?**

A Sand-wiches.

Q What do you call a sneezing train?

A Ah-choo-choo.

Q How did the rabbit do in her first show on Broadway?

A She gave a hare-raising performance.

Some types of grouper fish are born as females and turn into males as they get older!

HA! HA! HA! HA! HA! HA! HA! HA! HA! HA! HA! HA!

The arctic fox's feet are covered in fur to protect them from ice and snow. It can endure temperatures as low as minus 58°F (-50°C).

Siamese cats are quite intelligent! They can be trained to fetch, retrieve, and even do tricks.

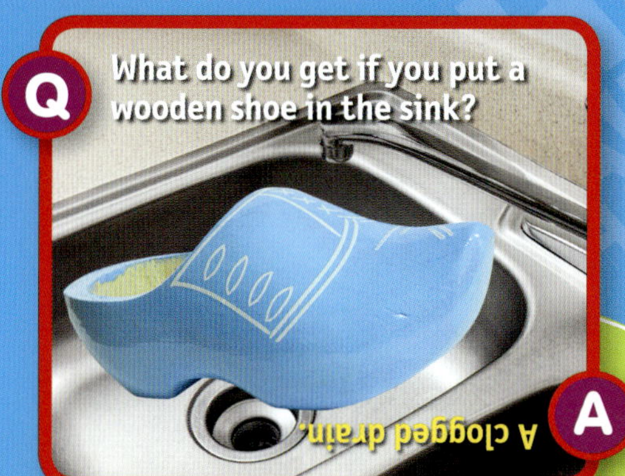

Q What do you get if you put a wooden shoe in the sink?

A

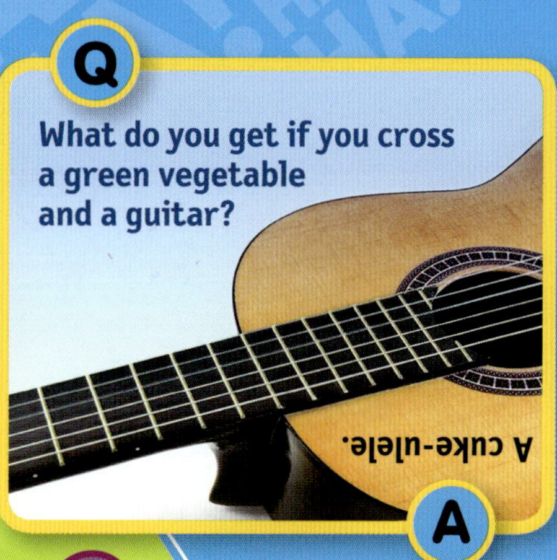

Q What do you get if you cross a green vegetable and a guitar?

A

Q What's worse than raining cats and dogs?

A

Q Why was the rock so frustrated?

A

Q
What do wildebeest yell on December 31?
A
Happy Gnu Year!

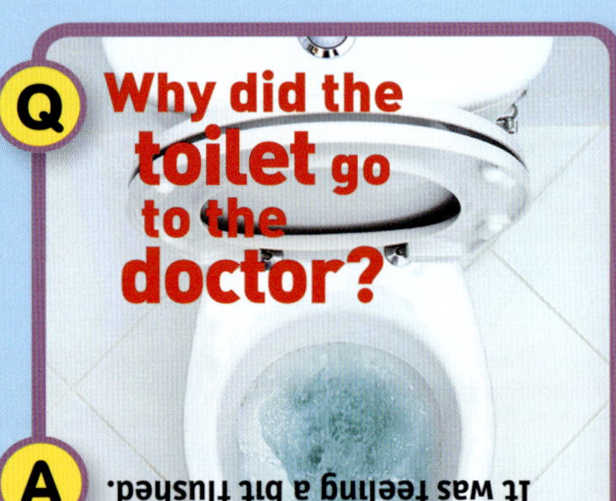

Q
Why did the toilet go to the doctor?
A
It was feeling a bit flushed.

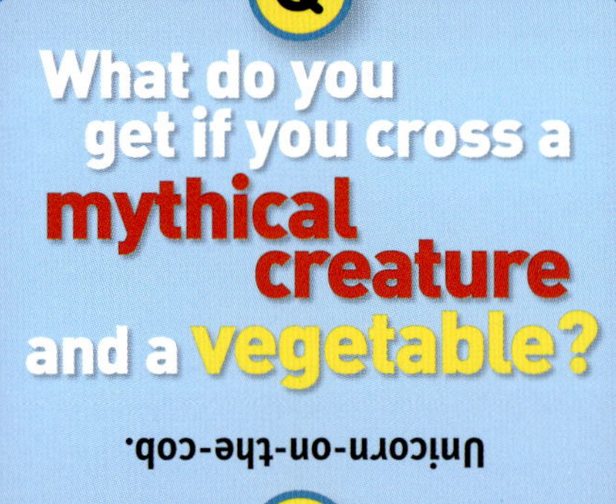

Q
What do you get if you cross a mythical creature and a vegetable?
A
Unicorn-on-the-cob.

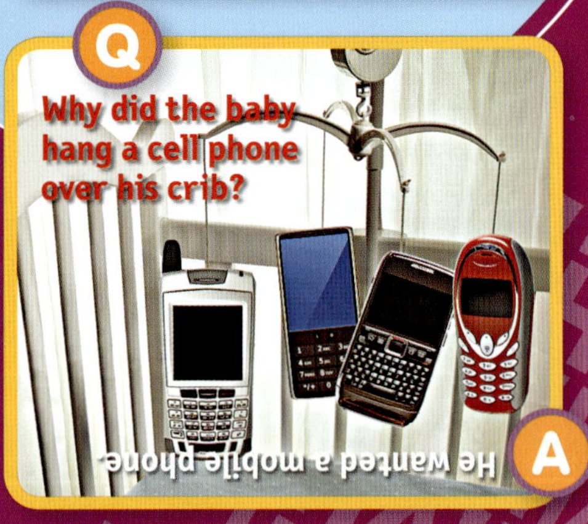

Q
Why did the baby hang a cell phone over his crib?
A
He wanted a mobile phone.

Giant Galápagos turtles can survive for up to a year without eating or drinking.
KNOCK, KNOCK.
Who's there?
Wanda.
Wanda who?
Wanda hear another joke?

He had a ruff day.

HA!HA!
HA!HA!
HA!HA!
HA!HA!
HA!HA!
HA!

KNOCK, KNOCK.
Who's there?
Yeast.
Yeast who?
You could at yeast open the door and say hello!

Q
What do you call a
potato that
joins a
monastery?
A
A chip monk.

Q
Why did the
man marry
a barbecue?
A
Because
it was the
grill of his
dreams.

Q

What do you get if you cross an emperor and a vegetable?

Genghis Corn.

A

Pelicans have air sacs in their bones to help them float on the water.
KNOCK, KNOCK.
Who's there?
Tibia.
Tibia who?
It's going tibia good day!

HA! HA! HA!
HA! HA! HA!

The red ruffed lemur gets its name from the ruff of fur around its neck.

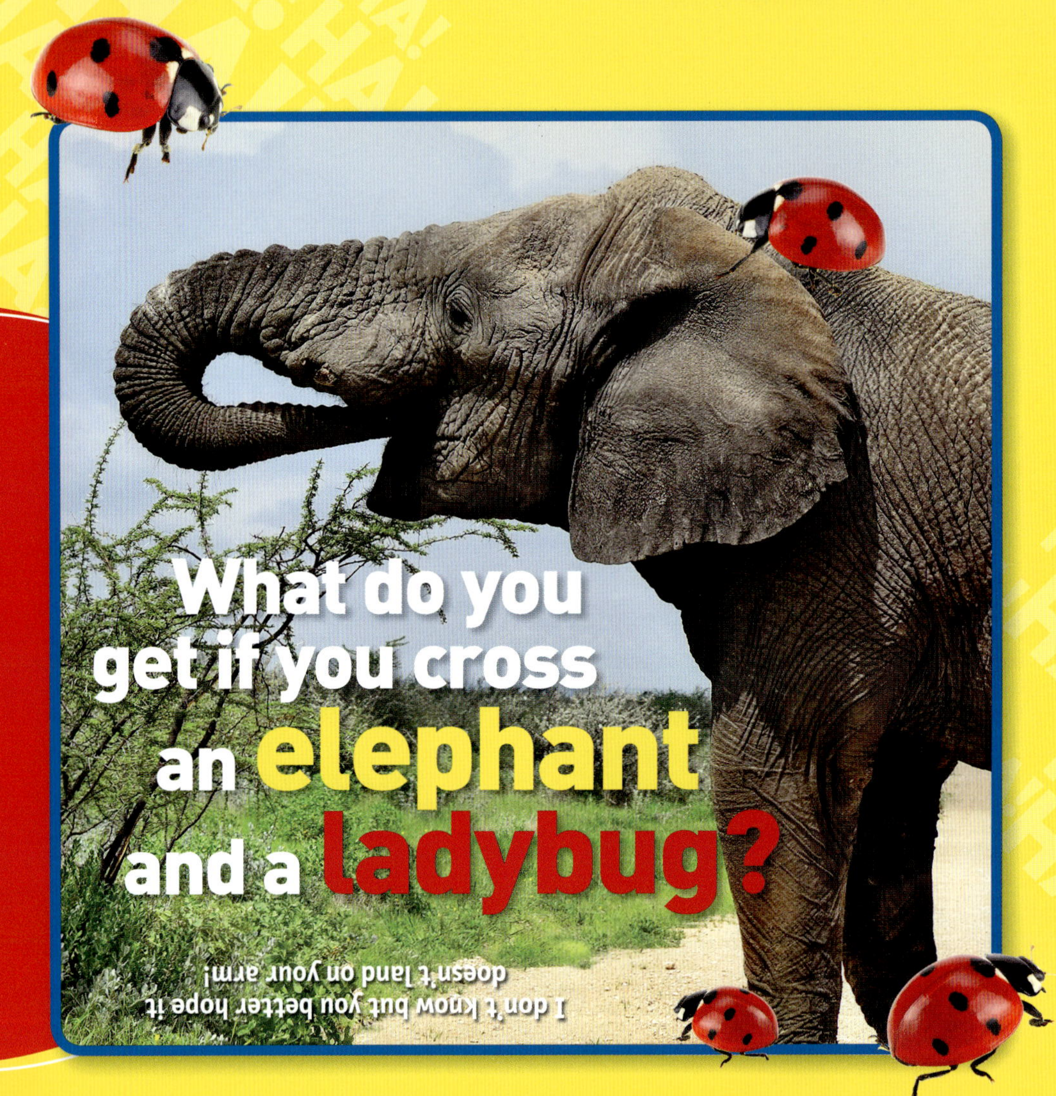

What do you
get if you cross
an elephant
and a ladybug?

I don't know but you better hope it
doesn't land on your arm!

FUNNY PUNS!

The giant boat sale was a big oar-deal!

Q
What did the bees do after they moved into their new hive?
A
They had a house-swarming party.

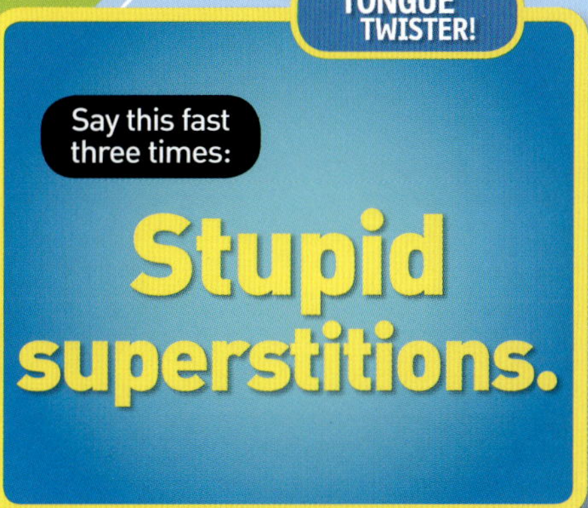
Q
Why should you never lie to an x-ray technician?
A
Because they can see right through you.

TONGUE TWISTER!
Say this fast three times:
Stupid superstitions.

Q Why is it fun to hang out with opera singers?

A Because they always leave you on a high note.

Q What is a **crocodile's** favorite **party game?**

A Swallow the leader.

Leftovers, anyone? A tiger will eat its kill until it is full and then hide it so it can return and continue eating when it is hungry again.

HA!
HA!
HA!
HA!
HA!
HA!
HA!
HA!
HA!
HA!

TONGUE TWISTER!

Say this fast three times:

Five frantic frogs
fled from fifty
fierce fishes.

What do pigs write letters with?
By air mail
Par avion
to:
Mr. Kevin Bacon
Hollywood, California
Pig pens.

CARRIE: Did you enjoy the tour of the cheese factory?

CHARLOTTE: A little bit cheesy, but I thought it was grate! Did you like it?

CARRIE: It could have been cheddar.

Killer whales live in groups called "pods."

Q What holiday do condiments celebrate?

A ¡Cinco de mayo!

Q Why did the orange join the navy?

A Because it was a naval orange.

KNOCK,
KNOCK.
Who's there?
Butter.
Butter who?
You butter be
ready to go!

Red foxes have excellent nighttime vision and do most of their hunting at night.

Q What is a **sea monster's** favorite dinner?

A Fish and ships.

Q Why did two coin collectors arrange a get-together?

A For old dimes' sake.

Q Why did the **comedian** stop at the **fabric store?**

A He was looking for new material.

How does a
seahorse
get from one place
to another
quickly?
Seahorses use their tails to grasp objects and anchor themselves in one place.
It scallops.

There are around 200 different species of owls. A group of owls is called a parliament.
KNOCK, KNOCK.
Who's there?
Penny.
Penny who?
Penny for your thoughts?

Did you hear about the guy who had a **bungee jumping** accident?

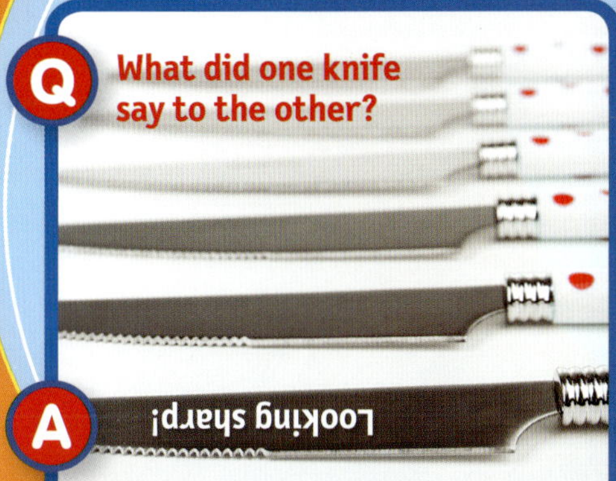

Don't be fooled by those short legs!
Basset hounds have powerful noses
and will give chase if they catch an
interesting scent.

Why did the dog bring a stick into the bank?
Because he was meeting the branch manager.

A baby great white shark is called a pup and can be up to 5 feet (1.5 m) long at birth.
KNOCK, KNOCK.
Who's there?
Whale.
Whale who?
I'm doing whale, how are you?

Q

A A mugging.

Q

What starts with a T, ends with a T, and is full of T?

A teapot.

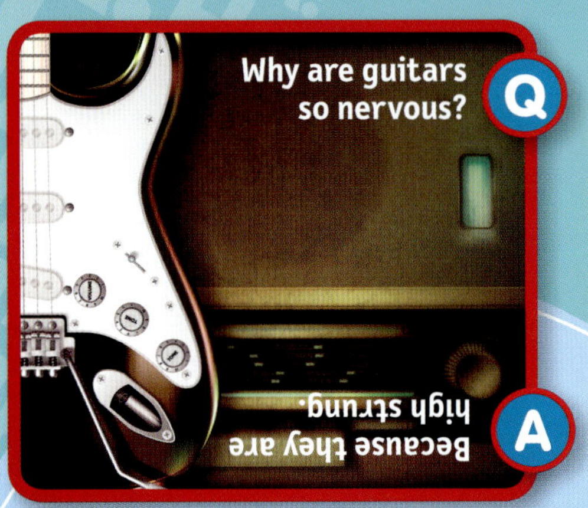

Why are guitars so nervous?
Q
Because they are high strung.
A

TONGUE TWISTER!
Say this fast three times:
Rough rafting rapids.

Q
What has to be broken before you can use it?
An egg.
A

What do you call a pig that can write with both hooves?
Q
Ham-bidextrous.
A

What did the
fish
name his
kid?
Gill.

HA!
HA!HA!
HA!HA!HA!
HA!HA!HA!
HA!HA!
HA!HA!
HA!

Draft horses are known for their tall stature and extremely muscular build. They can weigh up to 2,000 pounds (907 kg)!
KNOCK,
KNOCK.
Who's there?
Feline.
Feline who?
I'm feline a little cold, can I come in?

Wake up! A lion may sleep up to 20 hours a day.
KNOCK, KNOCK.
Who's there?
Thumping.
Thumping who?
Thumping green and thlimy is crawling up your leg!

Q

What has one horn and gives milk?

A A milk truck.

TONGUE TWISTER!

Say this fast three times:

Mrs. Smith's fish sauce shop.

Why shouldn't you play basketball with a pig?

There was a minimum of cinnamon.

It is believed that the female T. rex outweighed the male T. rex by a few thousand pounds.
KNOCK,
KNOCK.
Who's there?
Water.
Water who?
Water you doing? Can you come out and play?

What do you call a
sunbathing
grizzly?
A solar bear.

KNOCK, KNOCK.
Who's there?
Ogre.
Ogre who?
Thought I'd come ogre for a visit.

TONGUE TWISTER!
Say this fast three times:
Great Greek grape growers.

Q
Why are towels good comedians?

A
Because they have a dry sense of humor.

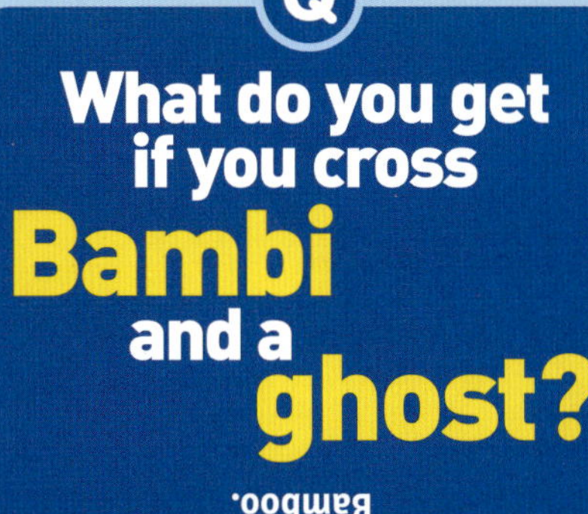

Q
What do you get if you cross Bambi and a ghost?
Bamboo.
A

CHEF:
How did you enjoy the soup?

DINER:
It was stew-pendous!

Q
How does Darth Vader like his toast?
On the dark side.
A

Q
Did the beluga have a good time at his birthday party?
He had a whale of a time!
A

TONGUE TWISTER!
Say this fast three times:
Mr. Meminger's editor's sweater.

Raccoons have long, delicate fingers and a highly sensitive sense of touch.
KNOCK,
KNOCK.
Who's there?
Watson.
Watson who?
Watson TV tonight?

INTERVIEWER:
What is your favorite letter of the alphabet?

PIRATE:
You may think it's arrrr, but my first love be the c.

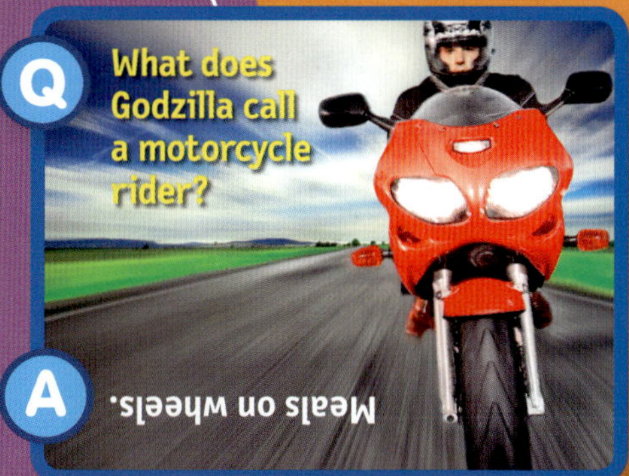

Bulldogs are one of the most popular mascots for universities and sports teams in the United States.

HA! HA! HA! HA!
HA! HA!
HA!
HA!
HA! HA!
HA! HA!
HA! HA!

What do you get if you cross **detergent** and a **talk show host?**

A

Q Why did the shoe join a dating service?

A He was looking for his sole mate.

What do **dogs** order in **restaurants?**

TONGUE TWISTER!
Say this fast three times:
Llamas lying lazily aloft a little log.

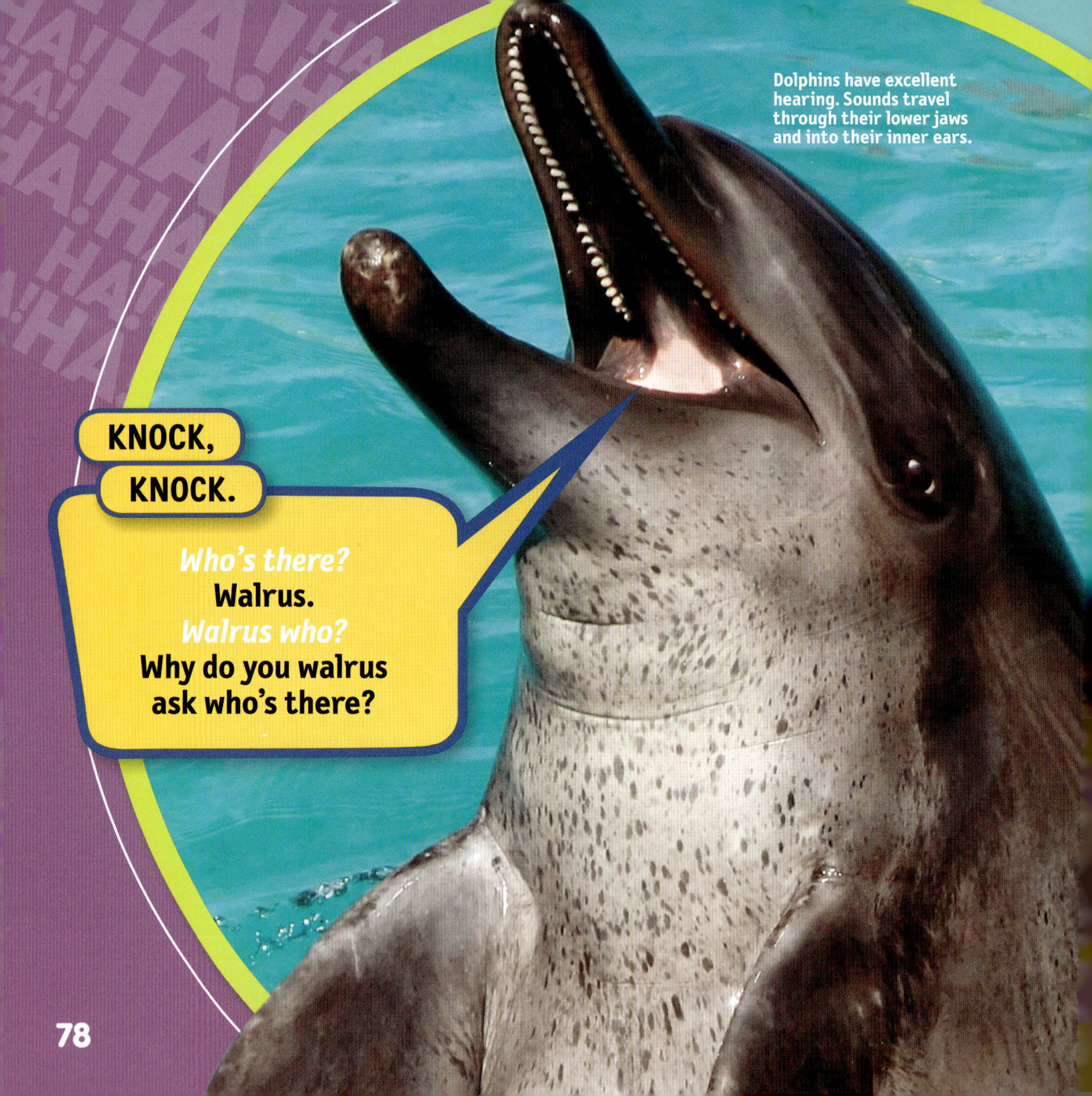

Dolphins have excellent hearing. Sounds travel through their lower jaws and into their inner ears.

Q What did one pumpkin say to the other pumpkin?
A Hey there gourd-geous!

TONGUE TWISTER!
Say this fast three times:
Bob brought the black boot back.

I really wanted a **camouflage shirt** but I couldn't find one.

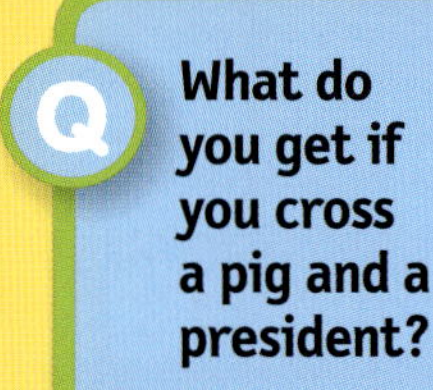

Baby robins are born with their eyes shut. They open around five days after hatching.
KNOCK,
KNOCK.
Who's there?
Henrietta.
Henrietta who?
Henrietta whole pizza and has a stomachache.

Catfish have whiskers called barbels. They use them to find food and feel their way around.
KNOCK, KNOCK.
Who's there?
Adam.
Adam who?
Up and Adam,
it's time to go!

HA!HA!
HA!HA!HA!
HA!HA!HA!
HA!HA!HA!
HA!HA!HA!
HA!HA!

Gray wolves are the largest members of the dog family. They can weigh up to 135 pounds (60 kg).

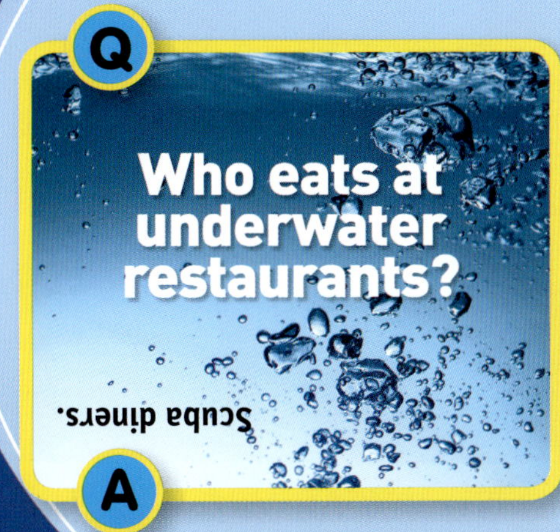

Q
Who eats at underwater restaurants?
A
Scuba diners.

Q How does music say goodbye?
A
Audios.

What happens if you hire a kitten to work in a Mexican restaurant?
Q
You get guaco-meowly on your furrito.
A

Q
What is a ghost's favorite holiday?
April Ghouls' Day.
A

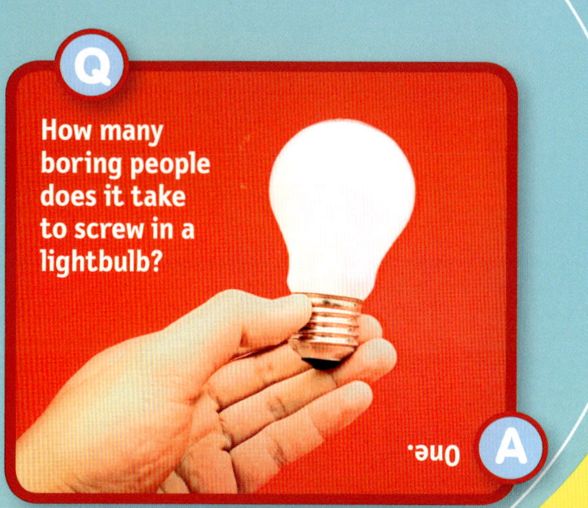

Q
How many boring people does it take to screw in a lightbulb?
A
One.

TONGUE TWISTER!
Say this fast three times:
Mad bunny, bad money.

KNOCK, KNOCK.
Who's there?
Alden.
Alden who?
When you're Alden with your homework, come out and play!

TONGUE
TWISTER!

Say this fast three times:
Flapjack Jack flipped flat flapjacks.

What do
cats
put on their
iPods?
10:25
Music
Photo
Video
FM Radio
Settings
Playlist
Meow-sic.
HA! HA! HA! HA! HA! HA! HA! HA!

Q
What do you call a skeleton that won't do his chores?
A
Lazy bones.

Q
What kind of snacks does a computer eat?
A
Microchips.

Q
What do you call a loaf of bread acting silly?
A
A weirdough.

TONGUE TWISTER!
Say this fast three times:
Santa's short suit shrunk.

It was a terrible summer for Humpty Dumpty, but he had a great fall.

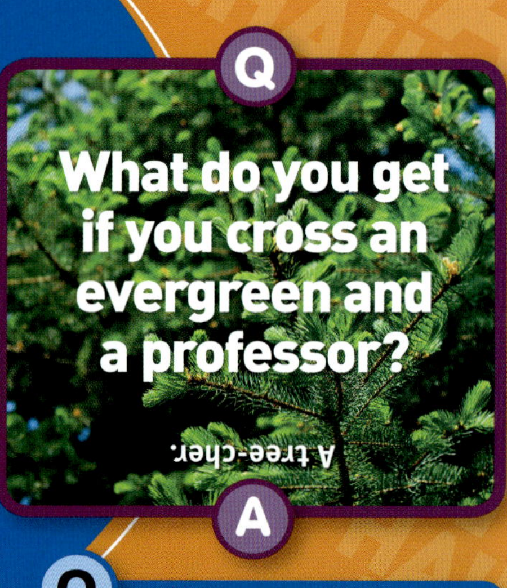

What do you get if you cross a pie and an ape?
A meringue-utan.

The closest relatives to hippos are cetaceans such as whales and dolphins.

HA!HA!HA!HA!HA!
HA!HA!HA!
HA!HA!
HA!HA!
HA!
HA!HA!
HA!HA!
HA!HA!HA!

Why do no two **female sheep** look alike?

Because each one is ewe-nique.

HELLO
my name is
DOLLY

Sloth bears feed on termites, honeybees, and fruit.

Why did the baker stop making donuts?
Q
A
She got tired of the hole thing.

TONGUE TWISTER!
Say this fast three times:
Ghost hosts boast the most.

Q
What is a ghost's favorite meal?
A
(Boo-ghum.)

TONGUE TWISTER!
Say this fast three times:
Swim, swam, swum.

Q
What do you get if you cross a pig and a cactus?
A
A porker-pine.

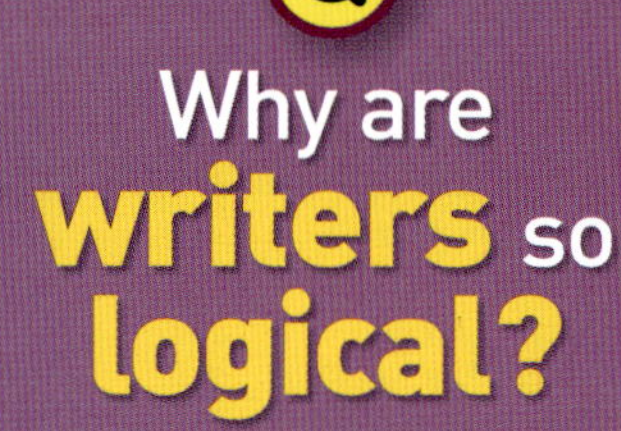
Q
Why are writers so logical?
A
Because they have a lot of comma sense.

A zebra's stripe pattern is as unique as a human's fingerprint.
KNOCK, KNOCK.
Who's there?
Eddie.
Eddie who?
Eddie body want to hear a knock-knock joke?

What do get if you cross a *T. rex* and a lemon?

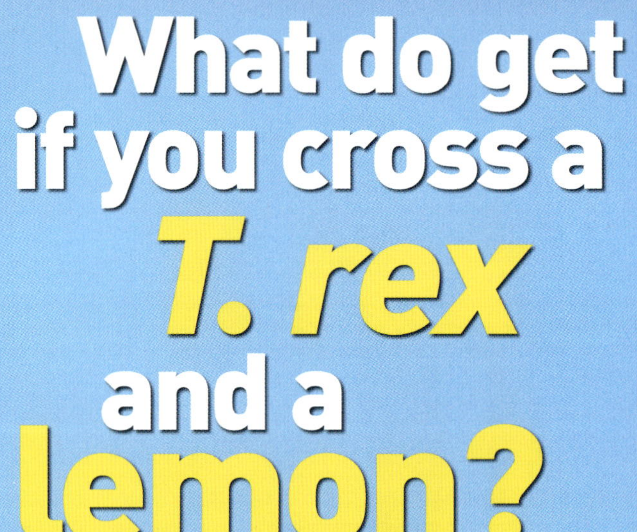

HA! HA! HA!
A dino-sour.
HA! HA! HA!

After a cheetah chases down its dinner, it needs half an hour to catch its breath before eating.

104

Q Why did the tiny pepper put on a sweater?

A He was a little chili.

Q

What **sport** does **Bigfoot** like to play?

A Sas-squash.

TONGUE TWISTER!

Say this fast three times:

Crisp crusts crackle crunchily.

Q What do you call a shark giving presents?

A Santa Jaws.

Q What do you get if you cross a cow and an octopus?

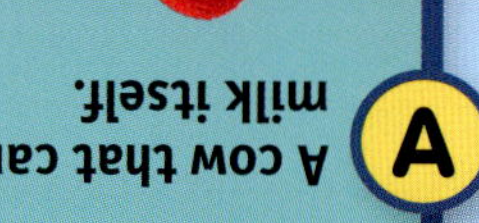

A A cow that can milk itself.

Q What kind of bugs live in an apartment?

A Ten-ants.

Q

What has a **neck** **but no** **head?**

A A bottle.

Which barnyard animal can sing and dance?
Justin Timberlamb.

Only the males are called peacocks. The females are called peahens!

What kind of car does an insect drive?
Q
A
A Volkswagen Beetle.

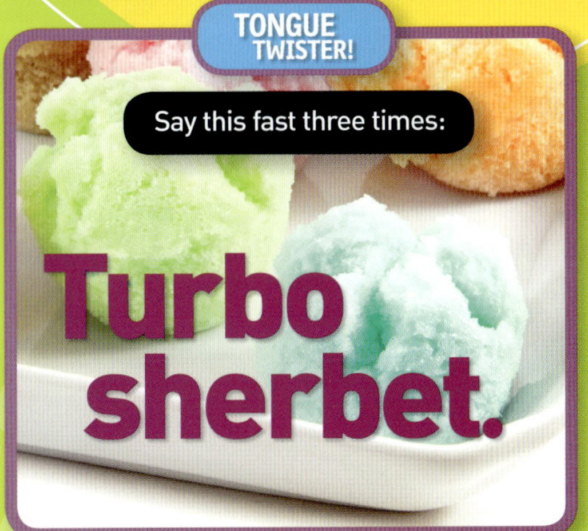

TONGUE TWISTER!
Say this fast three times:
Turbo sherbet.

KNOCK,
KNOCK.
Who's there?
Butternut.
Butternut who?
Butternut be late
for the movie.

American alligators have upward-facing nostrils that let them breathe while the rest of their body is underwater.

What do you get if you cross two snakes and a car window?
Q
A
Windshield vipers.

Q
What kind of band do killer whales play in?
A
An orca-stra.

I spy with my little eye ...
The lynx has excellent vision.
It can spot prey from 250 feet
(75 m) away.

What do you get if you cross a **shaggy dog** and a **couch?**

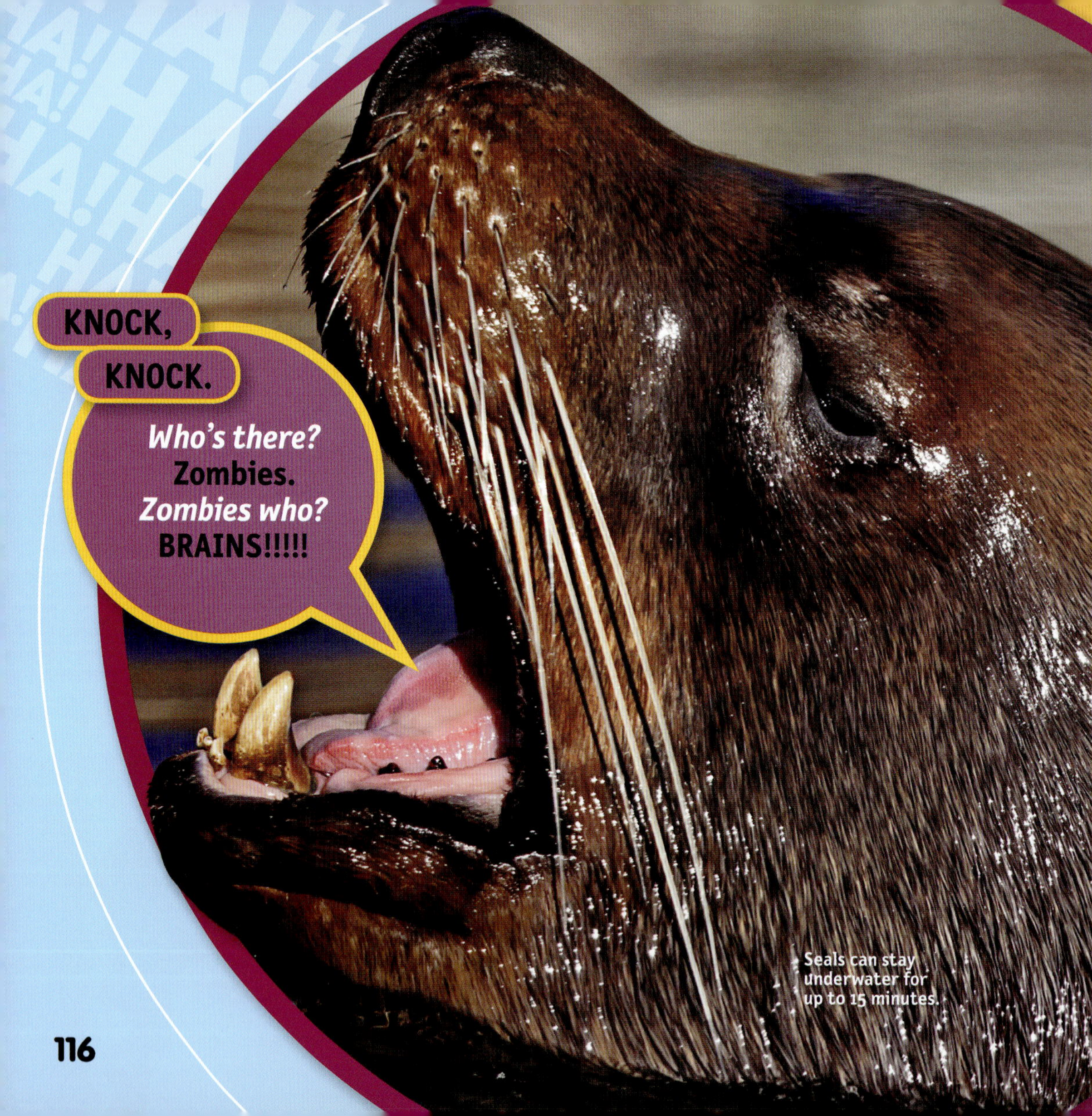
KNOCK, KNOCK.
Who's there?
Zombies.
Zombies who?
BRAINS!!!!!
Seals can stay underwater for up to 15 minutes.

TONGUE TWISTER!

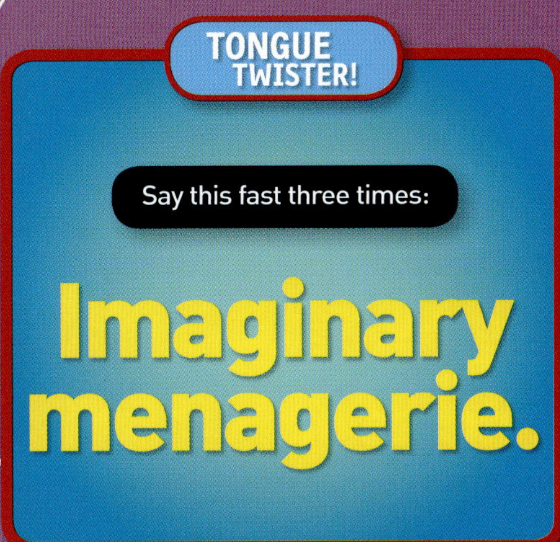

Say this fast three times:
Imaginary menagerie.

Q What gets wet while it is drying?
A towel. A

Q

What did one *font* say to the other *font*?

You are just my type!

A

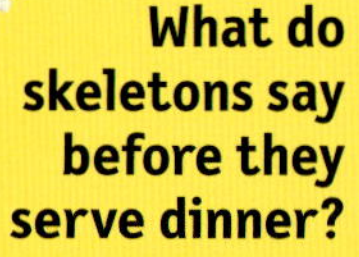

Where do fish post their photographs?
On Fin-stagram.

Gorillas are very intelligent.
Some have even learned
sign language!

KNOCK, KNOCK.
Who's there?
Ocelot.
Ocelot who?
You ocelot of questions.

When an elephant is thirsty, it can suck around 2 gallons (7.5 L) of water into its trunk to spray down its throat to drink.
KNOCK, KNOCK.
Who's there?
House.
House who?
House about we go for a walk?

LISA:

Hey! Someone stole my recliner!

FRED:

I couldn't chair less.

Q

What do you get
if you cross a
superhero
and a
box of **cereal?**

A

Iron Bran.

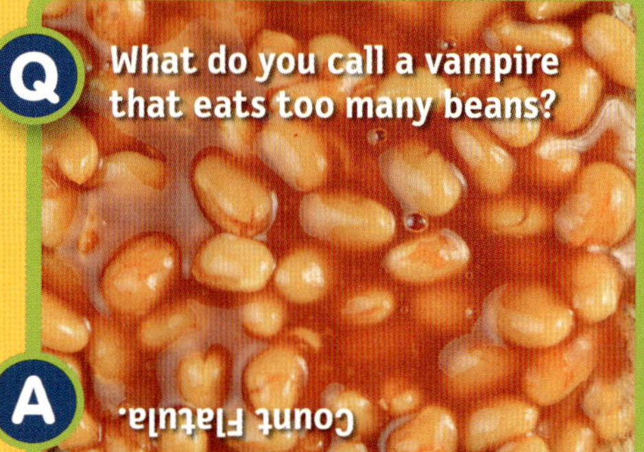

TONGUE TWISTER!

Say this fast three times:

Mimicking my hiccupping.

What do dogs like to eat for breakfast?
Barkon and woofles.

Why do
polar
bears have
fur coats?

Because they would look silly in sweaters.

A horse's eyes are on the sides of its head. Horses can see almost 360 degrees around themselves!
KNOCK, KNOCK.
Who's there?
Annie.
Annie who?
Annie one going to open the door?

What kind of **animal** **works** at the **bank?**

A loan wolf.

TONGUE TWISTER!

Say this fast three times:

Cheap ship trip.

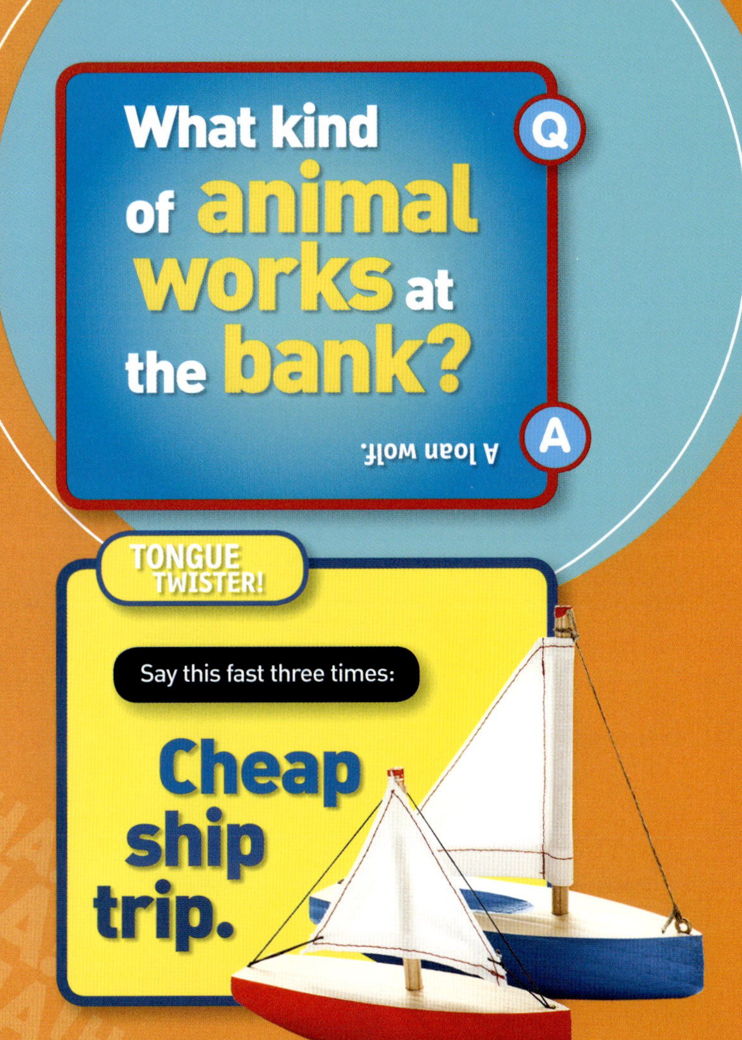

SPIDER 1:
Hey, do you like my new web?
SPIDER 2:
It's unbe-weave-able!

Q What football position do dogs play?
A Wide retriever.

Q What's the best side of the house to build a porch on?
A The outside.

Bald eagles have been the national symbol of the United States since 1782.

KNOCK,
KNOCK.

Who's there?
Carmen.
Carmen who?
Carmen see for yourself!

Look out! A skunk can spray its scent up to 12 feet (3.7 m) away!
KNOCK, KNOCK.
Who's there?
Randy.
Randy who?
Randy marathon and boy am I tired!

TONGUE TWISTER!

Say this fast three times:

Chester chews a chunk of cheap cheddar cheese.

Q How do prisoners phone each other?
A On their cell phones.

Q Did you hear about the new Mexican restaurant?
A It's the taco the town.

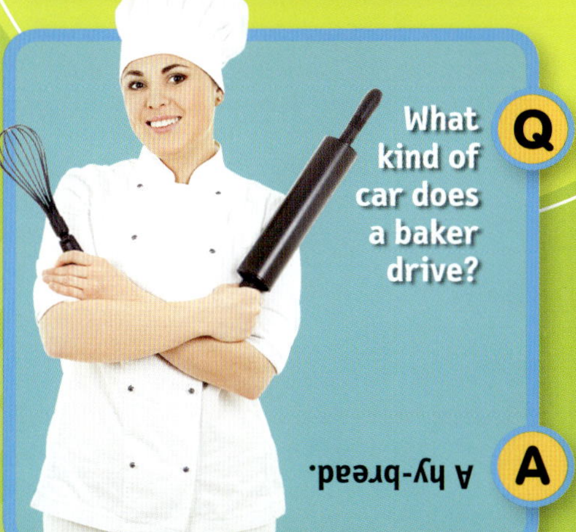

Q What kind of car does a baker drive?
A A hy-bread.

Q What kind of band plays snappy music?
A A rubber band.

TONGUE TWISTER!
Say this fast three times:
Real rural walrus.

Q What kind of medicine do you give a sick bed?
A Pill-os.

KNOCK, KNOCK.
Who's there?
Letters.
Letters who?
Letters in, it's dark out here!

What do you call a **surprised turtle?**

HONK! Canada geese call to each other with loud honks while flying.
KNOCK, KNOCK.
Who's there?
Gretta.
Gretta who?
Gretta move on, we are going to be late!

Q
Why did the chef go to jail?
A
He was caught beating an egg.
47A589   POLICE DEPARTMENT
MUGSHOT
HT 6'3" WT 163 DOB 07.12.1989
Q
What do you get if you cross a wizard and a horse?
A
Harry Trotter.
Q
Why did the hockey coach put a dog on the ice?
A
They needed a rufferee.
Q
Why don't chemists like to tell jokes?
A
Because they don't get a reaction.

Q
What did one steak say to the other?
A
So, we meat again.

Q
What do you get if you cross a dinosaur and a hot beverage?
A
Tea-Rex.

Q
What happened to the corn when it didn't do its homework?
A
It got an earful from its teacher.

Q
Which superhero likes to argue?
A
Spatman.

What is an egg's favorite horror movie?
The Eggsorcist.

Puffer fish aren't very good swimmers. They suck up water and "puff up" like a balloon to protect themselves from predators they are too slow to swim away from.
KNOCK, KNOCK.
Who's there?
Luke.
Luke who?
Luke through the peephole and find out!
HA! HA! HA! HA! HA! HA! HA! HA!

HA! HA! HA!
HA! HA! HA!
HA! HA! HA!
HA! HA! HA!
HA! HA! HA!
HA! HA!
HA! HA!
HA! HA! HA!
HA! HA! HA!
HA! HA! HA!
HA! HA! HA!

What kind of fruit has a bad attitude?
A grizzly pear.

KNOCK, KNOCK.
Who's there?
Jess.
Jess who?
Jess got here, did
I miss anything?

148

TONGUE TWISTER!
Say this fast three times:
Higgledy-piggledy.
What kind of watch does a witch wear?
Q
A Time-hex.
A

Q What kind of tests do chickens take?
A Egg-sams.

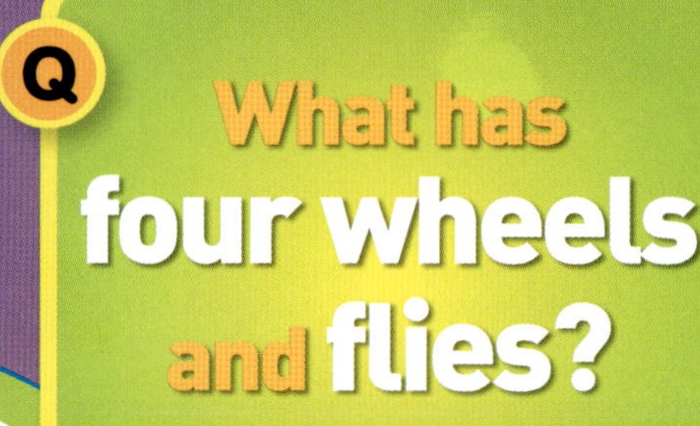

Q What has four wheels and flies?
A A garbage truck.

Q Why did the customer try to pay for his car with feathers?
A He heard he had to make a down payment.

TONGUE TWISTER!
Say this fast three times:
Eleven excited elves exchanged expensive earrings.

To get a long little doggy!

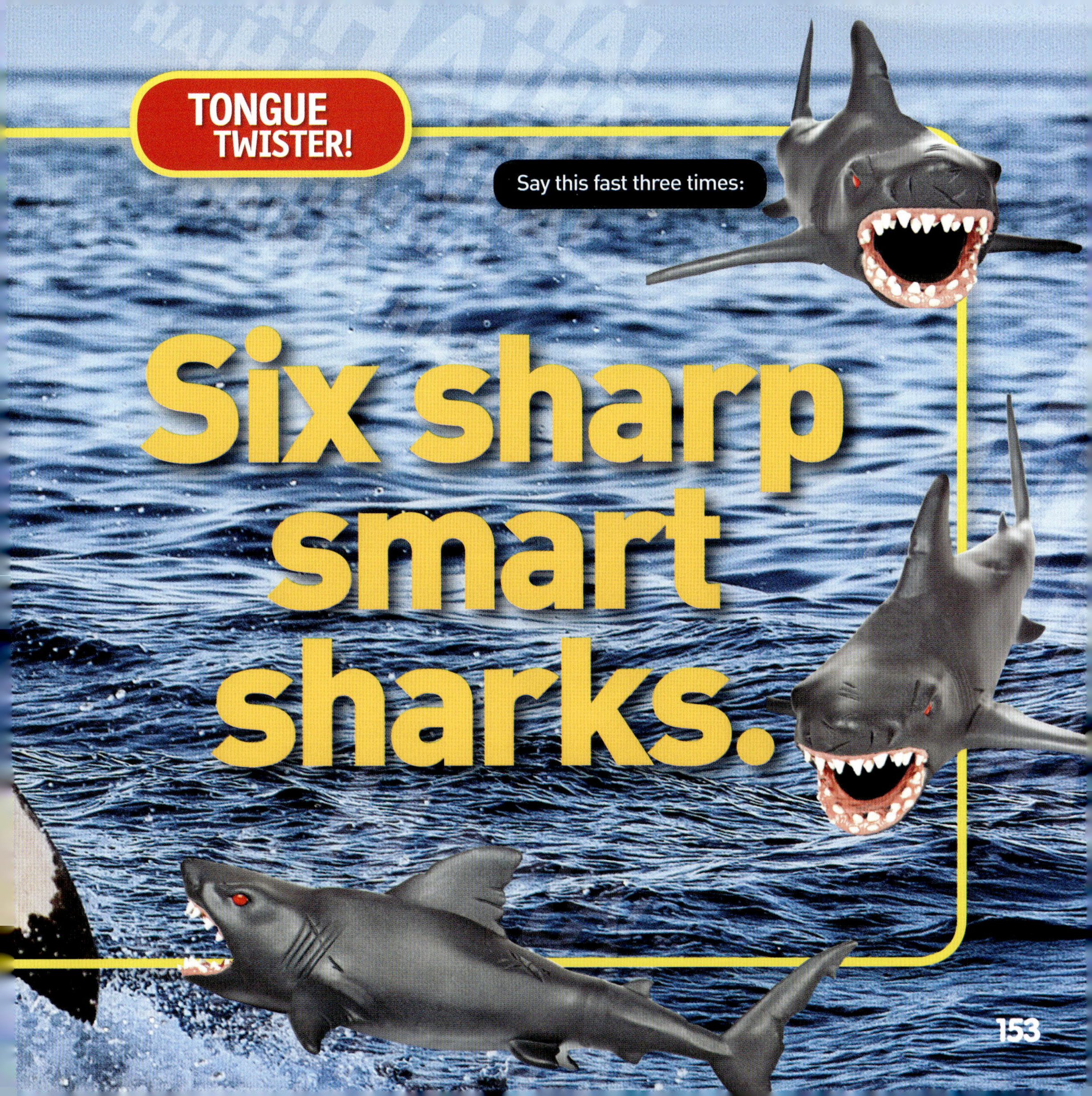

TONGUE TWISTER!
Say this fast three times:
Six sharp smart sharks.
153

The spectacled langur monkey is named for the white circles around its eyes that look like glasses.

Q What should you do with deviled eggs?

A Give them an eggs-orcism.

Q What shoes do ghosts wear when it's cold?

A Booots.

Q Why should you never lend your neighbor a rake?
A Because they will always come back for mower.

Q What did the jar of paste do on January 1?

A It made a Glue Year's resolution.

Q Which superhero works in an ice cream shop?
A Scooper-man.

Q What do you get if you cross a car and a famous Paris cathedral?

A The Hatchback of Notre Dame.

There are around 30 different types of terriers. They range in size from 2 to 70 pounds (1 to 32 kg).

Looks like trouble! A group of goldfish is called a troubling.

TONGUE TWISTER!
Say this fast three times:
Bungled burger burglary.

Q

What has two claws, four wheels, and a meter?

A

A taxi crab.

Q

What's the only coat you put on wet?

A

A coat of paint.

Q

What do you get if you cross a cow and a duck?

A

Milk and quackers.

Q

What kind of jokes do farmers like?

A

Corny ones.

Q How does the car muffler feel when it gets home?
A Exhausted.

Q What do you call a horse that is starring in a play?
A The mane attraction.

Only adult male cardinals have the distinctive red plumage. Females and babies are brown or gray with hints of red.

TONGUE TWISTER!
Say this fast three times:
Feathered finches flinch while flying forward fast.
164

Finches live on every
continent in the world
except Antarctica
and Australia.

A monitor lizard can dislocate a bone in its throat so it can swallow its food whole.

TONGUE TWISTER!
Say this fast three times:
Six slim sycamore saplings.

Q
What do you get if you cross a lamb and Japanese food?
A
Su-sheep.

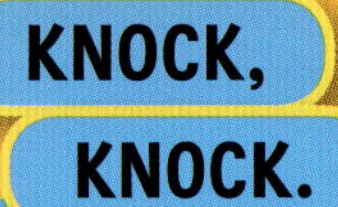

The blue and green macaw can live up to 50 years.

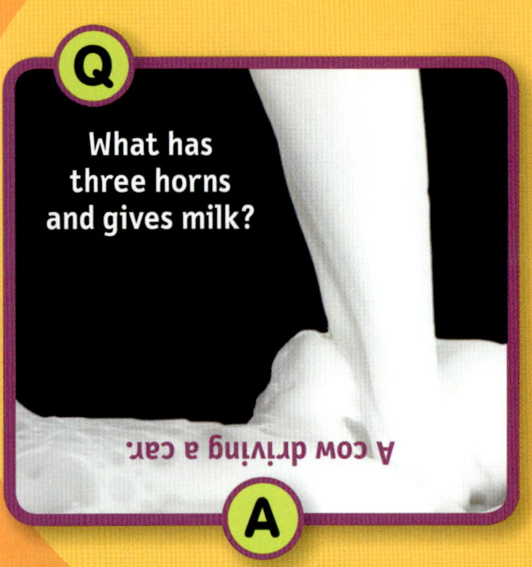
Q
What has
three horns
and gives milk?
A cow driving a car.
A

FUNNY PUNS!
Will February March? No, but April May.

What do you call a dinosaur that takes care of its teeth?
Q
A floss-iraptor.
A

Q
Did you hear about the fruit truck that crashed on the highway?
It created a traffic jam.
A

TONGUE TWISTER!
Say this fast three times:
Sick salamanders sipped and slurped soup.

What do you call a nut
with facial hair?
A mustachio.

Q
What do Dracula and a lollipop have in common?
A
They are both suckers.

TONGUE TWISTER!
Say this fast three times:
Hordes of Nords stormed the fjords.

Q
What kind of truck does a pig drive?
A
An 18-squealer.

Q
What did Darth Vader name his daughter?
A
Ella Vader.

Q What kind of creature lives in your keyboard?
A The Caps Lock Ness Monster.
Q How does a handyman get to school?
A On the tool bus.
Q What did one cleaver say to the other?
A Knife to meet you.
Q What kind of shoes would you find at a gas station?
A Gas pumps.

Goats do not like to get wet and will seek shelter when it is raining.

KNOCK, KNOCK.

Who's there?
Jewel.
Jewel who?
Jewel remember me when you see my face.

175

Where do fish go on vacation?
Fin-land.

KNOCK, KNOCK.
Who's there?
Harmony.
Harmony who?
Harmony more knock-knock jokes do you want to hear?
When hibernating, a bear's heart rate can fall from 40 beats a minute to 8 beats a minute.

Why did the dog go to the bank?
Q
A
To make a de-paws-it.

Q
What did one fish that was caught in a net say to the other?
A
Well, this is a fine mesh you got us into!

Why shouldn't you play cards with a hard-boiled egg?
Q
A
It is hard to beat.
GIRL 1:
Want to go shopping with me?
GIRL 2:
Nah, seen one shopping center, you've seen a mall.
TONGUE TWISTER!
Say this fast three times:
Thin sticks, thick bricks.

Chimpanzees are more closely related to humans than to gorillas or orangutans.

KNOCK, KNOCK.
Who's there?
Kanga.
Kanga who?
No, it's called a kangaROO.

Mummified remains of
Chihuahuas have been
found in Mesoamerican
grave sites. It was believed
that these little dogs helped
the owners travel to the
afterlife safely.

HA! HA!
HA! HA! HA!
HA! HA! HA! HA!

183

What do you get if you cross a sad dog and a fruit salad?
A melon collie.

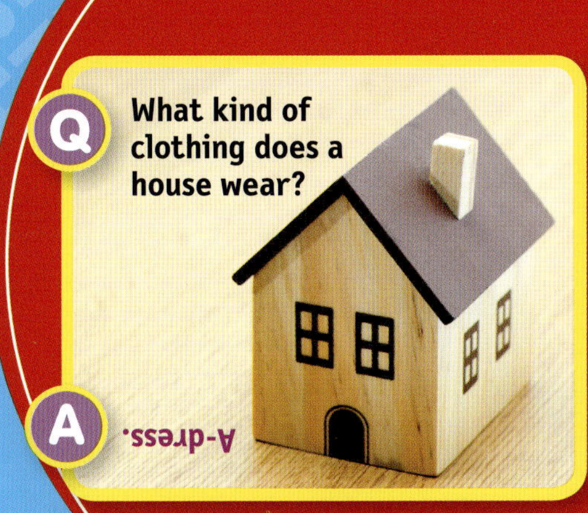

Q
What kind of clothing does a house wear?
A
A-dress.

ELLEN:
How do you like your soft drink?
JIM:
It is soda-licious!

TONGUE TWISTER!
Say this fast three times:
Shelley sells shades.

Q
Did you hear about the fire at the shoe factory?
One hundred soles were lost.
A

Q What is **1,450 feet (440 m) tall** and drinks **blood?**

A The Vampire State Building.

Q What kind of cell phone do you buy at a fruit stand?

A A Blackberry.

Kookaburras make loud, long calls that sound like laughter.

TONGUE TWISTER!

Double bubble gum trouble.

Hyenas live in large groups called clans. There can be up to 80 hyenas in a clan.
KNOCK, KNOCK.
Who's there?
Viper.
Viper who?
Viper feet, your shoes are wet.

Why is a frog always happy?
It eats whatever bugs him.

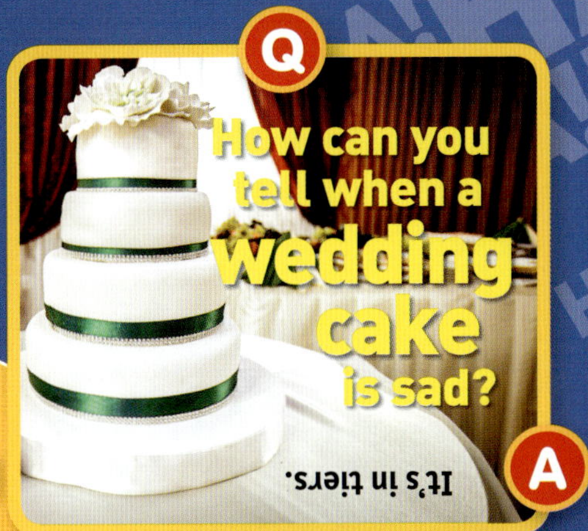
How can you tell when a wedding cake is sad?
It's in tiers.

What do you get if you cross a singer and an herb?
Elvis Parsley.

CROCODILE 1:
Did you have a good time at the comedy club?
CROCODILE 2:
I was croc-ing up laughing!

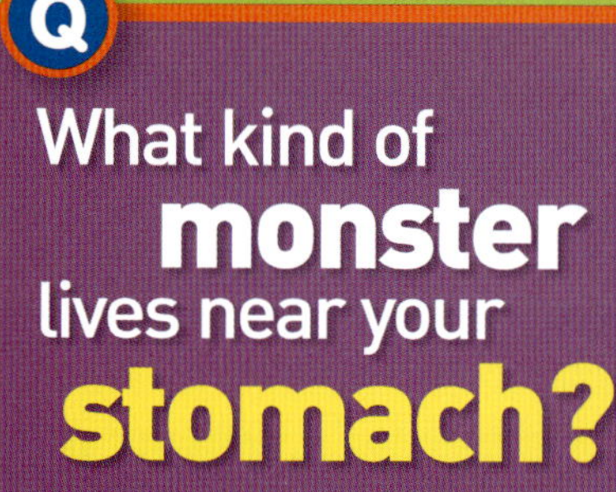

Q
What kind of **monster** lives near your **stomach?**
A
The abdominal snowman.

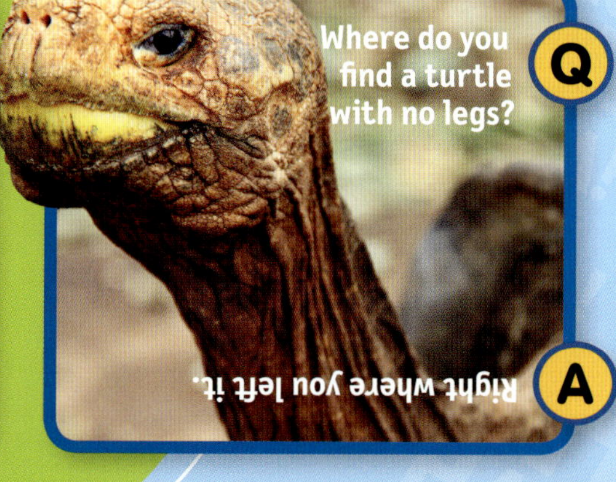

Q
Where do you find a turtle with no legs?
A
Right where you left it.

TONGUE TWISTER!
Say this fast three times:
Thistle-sifter.

Q
What do you get if you cross a frog and an automobile?
A
A car that can jump-start itself.

Penguins produce a waterproofing oil that they spread all over their bodies.
KNOCK, KNOCK.
Who's there?
Noah.
Noah who?
I Noah lot more jokes!

Sometimes dogs have two different-colored eyes. This is called heterochromia.

KNOCK,
KNOCK.
Who's there?
Pencil.
Pencil who?
Your pencil fall
down if you don't
wear a belt.

A group of
ring-tailed
lemurs is
called a troop.
KNOCK,
KNOCK.
Who's there?
Radio.
Radio who?
Radio not,
here I come!

SLUG 1: Hey, how do you think you did on our math test?
SLUG 2: I snailed it!

TONGUE TWISTER!
Say this fast three times:
Miss Mix picks chicks.

TONGUE TWISTER!
Say this fast three times:
Sixish.
Sixish.
Sixish.
Q
What do witches use to style their hair?
Scare spray.
A
What kind of ghost haunts a chicken coop?
Q
A poultry-geist.
A

What is a
kitten's
favorite
day
of the
week?
Cat-urday.

KNOCK,
KNOCK.
Who's there?
Peas.
Peas who?
Peas tell me there are no more knock-knock jokes!

Giant pandas are one of the world's rarest animals. There are only about 1,000 living in the wild.

Now
that
was
funny!

Question-and-answer jokes

Story jokes

Tongue twisters

ILLUSTRATION CREDITS

Credit Abbreviations:
DRMS: Dreamstime.com
SS: Shutterstock

Cover: Lynne M. Stone/Nature Picture Library
Back Cover: left, WilleeCole Photography/SS; right, Kentoh/SS

4-5 Otto Duplessis/DRMS; 6 Kamonrat/SS; 7 (bottom, right), Dan Kosmayer/SS; 8 (bottom, letter) Chris Brignell/SS; 8 (bottom, left), Pakhnyushcha/SS; 8 (top, right), Claudia Paulussen/SS; 8 (top, left), M. Unal Ozmen/SS; 9, Glitterd/DRMS; 10, Eric Isselee/SS; 12 (bottom, left), Sergey Uryadnikov/SS; 12 (bottom, left), Reika/SS; 12 (top, left), Nuttapong Wongcheronkit/SS; 13, Chrwarford/DRMS; 14, Anna IA/SS; 14 (up, right), AnnaIA/SS; 15 (bottom, left), Brent Hofacker/SS; 15 (bottom, left), Anest/SS; 15 (up, right), Aleksey Stemmer/SS; 15 (up, left), Waseef Akhtar/SS; 16, Leung Chopan/SS; 16 (left), Nagel Photography/SS; 18, Eric Gevaert/SS; 19 (bottom, right), Petruk Viktor/SS; 19 (top, right), Bildagentur Zoonar Gmbh/SS; 20 (bottom, left), World Pictures/SS; 20 (bottom, right), kak2s/SS; 20 (bottom, right), Steshkin Yevgeniy/SS; 20 (bottom, right), Peshkova/SS; 20 (top, left), Southern Light Studios/SS; 20 (top, right), Maxal Tamor/SS; 20 (top, left), Vinnikava Viktoryia/SS; 21, Amanda Nicholls/DRMS; 22-23, Isselee/DRMS; 24, Ilka Burckhardt/DRMS; 25 (bottom, left), Garsya/SS: 25 (bottom, right), Prill/SS; 25 (top, left), Michiel de Wit/SS; 25 (top, left), Carolyn Franks/SS; 25 (top, right), Fotoret/SS; 26 (bottom, right), Carsten Reisinger/SS; 26 (bottom, right), Nexus 7/SS; 26 (bottom, right), AdStock RF/SS; 26 (bottom, right), Ziviani/SS; 26 (top, right), Pyshnyy Maxim Vjacheslavovich/SS; 26 (top, left), Tarik Vision/SS; 29 (top, right), Rasulov/SS; 27, Marlene Frazier/DRMS; 28-29, Ysbrand Cosijn/SS; 30, GeNik/SS; 31 (bottom, right), Elnur/SS; 31 (bottom, right) Christian Delbert/SS; 31 (bottom, right), Tassel78/SS; 31 (bottom, right), Destiny Wedding Studio/SS; 31 (bottom, right), Daffodi Red/SS; 32 (bottom, left), R. Gino Santa Maria/SS; 32 (top, left), Jabiru/SS; 32 (top, right), Africa Studio/SS; 33 (top, right), Redfeniks/DRMS; 34, Eric Isselee/SS; 36, Karel Gallas/SS; 36 (top, left), Irin-k/SS; 37 (bottom, left), Its Me Just/SS; 37 (top, left), Elena Elisseeva/SS; 37 (top, right), Irin-k/SS; 37 (top, right), Tischenko Irina/SS; 38 (bottom, left), Susii/SS; 38 (top, left), Court Yard Pix/SS; 39, Anke Van Wyk/DRMS; 40, Maxim Tupikov/SS; 40 (bottom), Kuttelvaserova Stuchelova/SS; 42, S-F/SS; 42 (bottom), Ever/SS; 43 (bottom), Valentina_S/SS; 43 (bottom), Lissandra Melo/SS; 43 (top, left), Stockphoto-Graf/SS; 43 (top, right), Baibaz/SS; 44-45, David Pruter/DRMS; 45 (bottom, right), Aleksangel/SS; 45 (bottom, right), Happy Together/SS; 45 (top, right), Joe Belanger/SS; 45 (top, right), Lily 2014/SS; 46, Inna Astakhova/SS; 48 (bottom, left), Tom Gowanlock/SS; 48 (bottom, right), S_Photo/SS; 48 (top, left), Stasis Photo/SS; 48 (top, right), Triff/SS; 49, Bill Kennedy/SS; 50, Greenr/DRMS; 51 (bottom, left), Africa Studio/SS; 51 (bottom, right), Maria Starovoytova/SS; 51 (bottom, right), Svry/SS; 51 (top, right), Matthew Jacques/SS; 51 (top, right), Maxx-Studio/SS; 52-53, Ksenia Raykova/SS; 54, Paul Banton/DRMS; 55 (top, right), Svetlana Lukienko/SS; 56 (bottom, right), Bildagentur Zoonar GmbH/SS; 56 (top, left), Lem/SS; 56 (top, right), Strahil Dimitrov/SS; 57, Levent Konuk/SS; 58-59, Isselee/DRMS; 60, Jacoba Susanna Maria Swanepoel/DRMS 61 (bottom, left), Natali Zakharova/SS; 61 (bottom, right), Malgorzata Kistryn/SS; 61 (top, left), Christopher Elwell/SS; 62 (bottom, left), HandmadePictures/SS; 62 (top, left), Lasse Kristensen/SS; 62 (top, left), Tsekhmister/SS; 62 (top, left), Borislav Bajkic/SS; 62 (top, left), Irin-k/SS; 63, Leonello Calvetti/DRMS; 64, Gabriele Maltinti/SS; 64 (left), Volodymyr Burdiak/SS; 64 (top, left), Maris Kiselov/SS; 66, Eric Isselee/SS; 67 (bottom, right), Viritphon/SS; 67 (bottom, right), Dmytro Herasymeniuk/SS; 67 (top, right), Narisa Foto SS/SS; 68 (bottom, left), Home Art/SS; 68 (bottom, left), Luna Vandoorne Vallejo/DRMS; 68 (top, right), Sergey Mironov/SS; 69, Stokkete/SS; 70, NorthernLand/SS; 71 (bottom, left), Fun Way Illustration/SS; 71 (bottom, right), Ben Heys/SS; 71 (top, right), Smileus/SS; 72, Erik Lam/DRMS; 74 (bottom, left), Anueing/SS; 74 (bottom, right) Kucher Serhii/SS; 74 (bottom), Maglara/SS; 75 (top, right), Ksenia Merenkova/SS; 76, Som Photo/SS; 78, Duncan Noakes/DRMS; 79 (bottom), Indigo Lotos/SS; 79 (top), Chris Smart/SS; 80 (bottom, right), Eurobanks/SS; 80 (bottom, right), Tsekhmister/SS; 80 (top, right), Kathriba/SS; 80 (top, right), Clark Fang/SS; 80 (top, right), Lubava/SS; 81, Cheryl Davis/DRMS; 82, Youths/DRMS; 84, Ryan Jaime/DRMS; 85 (bottom, left), Miguel Garcia Saavedra/SS; 85 (bottom, left), Hannadarzy/SS; 85 (top, left), Olga Nikonova/SS; 85 (top, right), Jaboo 2foto/SS; 86 (bottom, left), Hannamariah/SS; 86 (top, left), Olaru Radian-Alexandru/SS; 87, Nagel Photography/SS; 88, Olga Miltsova/SS; 90 (left), Koldunov Alexey/SS; 90 (bottom, right), You can more/SS; 90 (top), Dr. Cloud/SS; 91 (bottom, left), RT Images/SS; 91 (bottom, left), Iryna Melnyk/SS; 91 (bottom, right), Luis Santos/SS; 91 (top, left), Kocetoiliev/SS; 91 (top, left), Valentyna Chukhlyebova/SS; 91 (top, right), Harvepino/SS; 92 (bottom, left), Chris Harvey/SS; 92 (bottom, right), Jonson/SS; 92 (top, right), Clear Images/SS; 93, Rob Hainer/SS; 93 (bottom), Istetiana/SS; 94, Eric Isselee/SS; 96, SomPhoto/SS; 96 (bottom), Mega Pixel/SS; 98, Brian Upton/SS; 99 (bottom, right), Jörg Röse-Oberreich/SS; 99 (top, right), Thirteen/SS; 100 (bottom, left), Micha Klootwijk/SS; 100 (top, left), Nikolai Tsvetkov/SS; 100 (top, left), Eurobanks/SS; 100 (top, left), S_Photo/SS; 100 (top, right), Romrf/SS; 101, Hammett79/SS;

102 (bottom), Africa Studio/SS; 103, Cuson/SS; 104, Maggy Meyer/SS; 105 (bottom, right), Kim Nguyen/SS; 105 (bottom, right), Elizabeth Hoffmann/SS; 105 (bottom, right), Kim Nguyen/SS; 105 (top, left), Ruslan Kudrin/SS; 105 (top, left), Maks Narodenko/SS; 106 (bottom, right), Aboikis/SS; 106 (bottom, right), Trenzy/SS; 106 (top, left), Channarong Meesuk/SS; 106 (top, left), Aa3/SS; 106 (top, right), Jessica Kirsh/SS; 107 (bottom, left), Montego/SS; 107 (right), Erik Lam/SS; 107 (right), Paket/SS; 107 (top, right), John Abbate/SS; 108, Nagel Photography/SS; 109 (bottom, right), Kentoh/SS; 109 (top, right), Andrey Pavlov/SS; 110, Robert Eastman/SS; 112 (bottom), Christopher Meder/SS; 112 (top), Christian Mueller/SS; 113, Michael Wick/SS; 114, Maria Kraynova/SS; 115, Eleana/SS; 116, Olga_gl/SS; 117 (bottom, right), Dzaky Murad/SS; 118 (bottom, right), RT Images/SS; 118 (bottom, right), Gen Epic Solutions/SS; 118 (top, right), R_Szatkowski/SS; 118 (top, right), Alexei Logvinovich/SS; 119, Motorolka/SS; 119 (bottom), Vasin Lee/SS; 120, Eric Isselee/DRMS; 122, Mark O'Flaherty/SS; 123 (left), Tovkach Oleg/SS; 123 (top, right), Dennis/SS; 124 (top, left), Panbazil/SS; 124 (top, right), Vetasster/SS; 124 (bottom, left), Anch/SS; 124 (bottom, left), Africa Studio/SS; 125 (bottom), Andrey_Kuzmin/SS; 125 (top), Annette Shaff/SS; 126, Cindy Creighton/SS; 128, Sari ONeal/SS; 129 (bottom, right), Jules Kitano/SS; 130 (left), Tetiana Yurchenko/SS; 130 (bottom, left), Karamysh/SS; 130 (top, right), WilleeCole Photography/SS; 131, Teri Virbickis/SS; 132, Eric Isselee/SS; 134, Southern Light Studios/SS; 135 (bottom, left), Diana Valujeva/SS; 135 (bottom, left), Val Lawless/SS; 135 (top, right), Bernd Juergens/SS; 136 (bottom, left), Atiketta Sangasaeng/SS; 136 (top, left), Aleksei Verhovski/SS; 137, Annette Shaff/SS; 138, Rusty Dodson/SS; 140, David P. Lewis/SS; 141 (bottom, left), zow/SS; 141 (bottom, right), Ralf Maassen (DTEurope)/SS; 141 (top, left), Africa Studio/SS; 141 (top, right), Chamille White/SS; 141 (top, right), Accept Photo/SS; 142 (bottom, left), Alexandra Lande/SS; 142 (top, left), Erwinova/SS; 142 (top, right), M. Unal Ozmen/SS; 142 (top, right), Andrea Ricordi/SS; 143, Boris Rabtsevich/SS; 143 (bottom, left), M. Unal Ozmen/SS; 143 (bottom, right), M. Unal Ozmen/SS; 144, Eric Isselee/SS; 146, Serg64/SS; 148, John Michael Evan Potter/SS; 149 (bottom, right), David Evison/SS; 149 (bottom, right), Nikuwka/SS; 149 (top, right), Evgeny Karandaev/SS; 150 (bottom, left), Shebeko/SS; 150 (bottom, right), Rustamir/SS; 150 (bottom, right), Rustamir/SS; 150 (top, left), Denis Nata/SS; 150 (top, left), Wikrom/SS; 151, Annette Shaff/SS; 152, Sergey Uryadnikov/SS; 152 (top), Juan Carlos Tinjaca/SS; 154, Palo_ok/SS; 155 (bottom, right), Debbie Vinci/SS; 155 (bottom, right), TerraceStudio/SS; 155 (bottom, right), Kucher Serhii/SS; 155 (bottom, right), Bonchan/SS; 156 (bottom, left), M. Unal Ozmen/SS; 156 (top, left), Africa Studio/SS; 156 (top, right), BW Folsom/SS; 157, Otsphoto/SS; 158 (bottom, left), ANP/SS; 158 (right), Vangert/SS; 160 (bottom, right), Africa Studio/SS; 160 (bottom, right), Indigolotos/SS; 160 (top), Primopiano/SS; 161 (bottom, left), Denis Nata/SS; 161 (bottom, left), Smereka/SS; 161 (bottom, right), John Kasawa/SS; 161 (top, left), Nykonchuk Oleksii/SS; 161 (top, right), Veerachai Viteeman/SS; 162 (bottom, left), Eric Isselee/SS; 162 (bottom, left), Repina Valeriya/SS; 162 (top, left), Freer/SS; 163, Charles Brutlag/DRMS; 164, Steven Russel lSmith Photos/SS; 166, Sprocky/SS; 167 (bottom, right), Phongsak Chartphet/SS; 167 (bottom, right), Marcelo_Krelling/SS; 167 (top, right), Jo Crebbin/SS; 168, Eric Isselee/SS; 170 (bottom, left), Willequet Manuel/SS; 170 (bottom, left), Macbrianmun/SS; 170 (bottom, right), Supot Suebwongsa/SS; 170 (top, left), Schankz/SS; 170 (top, right), David M. Schrader/SS; 171, Kazakov Maksim/SS; 171, Julia Sudnitskaya/SS; 172, Twonix Studio/SS; 172, Graletta/SS; 173 (bottom, left), Antpkr/SS; 173 (top, left), Svetlana Foote/SS; 173 (top, left), Paul Michael Hughes/SS; 173 (top, right), Strahil Dimitrov/SS; 174 (top, left), Jason Nemeth/SS; 174 (top, right), Africa Studio/SS; 174 (bottom, left), Africa Studio/SS; 174 (bottom, right), Apples Eyes Studio/SS; 175, Imageman/SS; 176, LauraD/SS; 176 (bottom), Africa Studio/SS; 177, BW Folsom/SS; 178, Pavel Kovacs/SS; 179 (top, right), Bullet74/SS; 179 (bottom, right), Puwanai/SS; 180 (bottom, right), Peter Gudella/SS; 180 (top, right), Africa Studio/SS; 180 (bottom, left), Dancestrokes/SS; 180 (top, left), Diana Valujeva/SS; 181, Pavel Kovacs/SS; 182, Andrey Kuzmin/DRMS; 184, Twilight Artistry/SS; 184 (bottom, left), Margouillat Photo/SS; 185 (top, left), Joel_420/SS; 185 (bottom, left), Hobbit/SS; 185 (top, right), Mahathir Mohd Yasin/SS; 185 (bottom, right), Anteromite/SS; 186 (bottom, left), Ad Stock RF/SS; 186 (bottom, left), Kryvenok Anastasiia/SS; 187, Shadow Mac/SS; 188, Marie C Fields/SS; 190, Bonga 1965/SS; 191 (top, left), Gaschwald/SS; 191 (bottom, left), Floydine/SS; 191 (bottom, right), Dave Montreuil/SS; 191 (top, right), Robert-Horvat/SS; 191 (bottom, left), Paco Toscano/SS; 191 (top, right), Jsbdueck/SS; 191 (bottom, right), Eric Isselee/SS; 191 (bottom, right), Nagy-Bagoly Arpad/SS; 193, Volodymyr Goinyk/SS; 194, Patryk Kosmider/SS; 196, Tao Jiang/SS; 197 (top, right), Lisa S./SS; 197 (top, right), QiuJu Song/SS; 197 (bottom, right), Volodymyr Burdiak/SS; 198 (bottom, left), Steve Collender/SS; 198 (bottom, right), Aksenova Natalya/SS; 198 (top, right), Oksana2010/SS; 199, Marlinde/SS; 200, Hung Chung Chih/SS;

Published by the National Geographic Society
Gary E. Knell, *President and Chief Executive Officer*
John M. Fahey, *Chairman of the Board*
Declan Moore, *Executive Vice President; President, Publishing and Travel*
Melina Gerosa Bellows, *Publisher and Chief Creative Officer,
    Books, Kids, and Family*

Prepared by the Book Division
Hector Sierra, *Senior Vice President and General Manager*
Nancy Laties Feresten, *Senior Vice President, Kids Publishing and Media*
Jennifer Emmett, *Vice President, Editorial Director, Kids Books*
Eva Absher-Schantz, *Design Director, Kids Publishing and Media*
Jay Sumner, *Director of Photography, Kids Publishing*
R. Gary Colbert, *Production Director*
Jennifer A. Thornton, *Director of Managing Editorial*

Staff for This Book
Shelby Alinsky, *Project Editor*
Julide Dengel, *Art Director*
Lisa Jewell, *Photo Editor*
Paige Towler, *Editorial Assistant*
Callie Broaddus, *Design Production Assistant*
Margaret Leist, *Photo Assistant*
Grace Hill, *Associate Managing Editor*
Mike O'Connor, *Production Editor*
Lewis R. Bassford, *Production Manager*
Susan Borke, *Legal and Business Affairs*

Production Services
Phillip L. Schlosser, *Senior Vice President*
Chris Brown, *Vice President, NG Book Manufacturing*
George Bounelis, *Senior Production Manager*
Nicole Elliott, *Director of Production*
Rachel Faulise, *Manager*
Robert L. Barr, *Manager*

Editorial, Design, and Production by Plan B Book Packagers

The National Geographic Society is one of the world's largest nonprofit scientific and educational organizations. Founded in 1888 to "increase and diffuse geographic knowledge," the Society's mission is to inspire people to care about the planet. It reaches more than 400 million people worldwide each month through its official journal, *National Geographic*, and other magazines; National Geographic Channel; television documentaries; music; radio; films; books; DVDs; maps; exhibitions; live events; school publishing programs; interactive media; and merchandise. National Geographic has funded more than 10,000 scientific research, conservation and exploration projects and supports an education program promoting geographic literacy.

For more information, please visit nationalgeographic.com,
call 1-800-NGS LINE (647-5463), or write to the following address:
National Geographic Society
1145 17th Street N.W.
Washington, D.C. 20036-4688 U.S.A.

Visit us online at nationalgeographic.com/books

For librarians and teachers: ngchildrensbooks.org

More for kids from National Geographic: kids.nationalgeographic.com

For information about special discounts for bulk purchases, please contact National Geographic Books Special Sales: ngspecsales@ngs.org

For rights or permissions inquiries, please contact National Geographic Books Subsidiary Rights: ngbookrights@ngs.org

Paperback ISBN: 978-1-4263-1735-4
Reinforced Library Binding ISBN: 978-1-4263-1736-1

Printed in China

15/PPS/1-BX